W9-CCD-692

Contents

When God's Spirit Moves

Six Sessions on the Life-Changing Power
of the Holy Spirit

PARTICIPANT'S GUIDE

Jim Cymbala

with Dean Merrill

ZONDERVAN®

ZONDERVAN.com/
AUTHORTRACKER
follow your favorite authors

ZONDERVAN

When God's Spirit Moves Participant's Guide
Copyright © 2011 by Jim Cymbala

Requests for information should be addressed to:
Zondervan, *Grand Rapids, Michigan 49530*

ISBN 978-0-310-32223-8

Published in association with the literary agency of Ann Spangler and Company, 1420 Pontiac Road S.E., Grand Rapids, MI 49506.

Cover design: Faceout Studio
Interior design: Sherri L. Hoffman

Printed in the United States of America

13 14 15 16 /DCI/ 24 23 22 21 20 19 18 17 16 15 14 13 12 11 10 9 8

When God's
Spirit Moves

Other Resources by Jim Cymbala

You Were Made for More (book and audio)
Fresh Wind, Fresh Fire (book and audio)
Fresh Faith (book and audio)
Fresh Power (book and audio)
Breakthrough Prayer (book and audio)
The Life God Blesses (book and audio)
The Church God Blesses (book and audio)
God's Grace from Ground Zero (book and audio)
When God's People Pray (video curriculum)

Agent in the Shadows

Jesus: "I will ask the Father, and he will give you another advocate to help you and be with you forever — the Spirit of truth. The world cannot accept him, because it neither sees him nor knows him. But you know him, for he lives with you and will be in you."

(John 14:16 – 17)

If you were teaching a class of seven-year-olds and had to explain the Holy Spirit and what he does, how would you go about it? What words would you use for these children? What examples?

Video Teaching Segment

Notes

As you watch the session one video, use the following outline to jot down any ideas that stand out to you.

Church life badly needs the Holy Spirit.

Jesus was leaving?

The Holy Spirit gets *inside* us.

The early apostles and the Holy Spirit

Current misgivings about the Holy Spirit

What the Spirit does *today*

The Roma Black story

1. Think of someone in your life who fills the role of *agent*—your car or home insurance agent, for example. What does this person do? How is that similar to what the Holy Spirit does in relation to the Godhead?

2. Read John 16:5 – 16 aloud:

   But now I am going to him who sent me. None of you asks me, "Where are you going?" Rather, you are filled with grief because I have said these things. But very truly I tell you, it is for your good that I am going away. Unless I go away, the Advocate will not come to you; but if I go, I will send him to you. When he comes, he will prove the world to be in the wrong about sin and righteousness and judgment: about sin, because people do not believe in me; about righteousness, because I am going to the Father, where you can see me no longer; and about judgment, because the prince of this world now stands condemned.

   I have much more to say to you, more than you can now bear. But when he, the Spirit of truth, comes, he will guide you into all the truth. He will not speak on his own; he will speak only what he hears, and he will tell you what is yet to come. He will glorify me because it is from me that he will receive what he will make known to you. All that belongs to the Father is mine. That is why I said the Spirit will receive from me what he will make known to you.

   In a little while you will see me no more, and then after a little while you will see me.

Here Jesus surprised his disciples by saying he would be leaving soon—and that would be a *good* thing for them. In what sense? If you had been present that evening in the Upper Room, would you have been convinced by Jesus' train of thought here? Why do you think Jesus said this?

3. Record what the following Scriptures say about things the Holy Spirit has done in our *past*.

   a. John 3:5–8

   b. Titus 3:5–7

   c. Romans 8:5–6

"Some people say, 'I don't want to know about the Holy Spirit; I just go by the Word.' But the Holy Spirit *wrote* the Word and speaks a lot about himself there."

From the video

4. Now record what the following Scriptures say about things the Holy Spirit wants to do in our *present*.

   a. John 14:26

   b. Romans 8:13–16

   c. 2 Timothy 1:6–7

5. Think back to the Roma Black story. How did the Holy Spirit show up as Roma sat in the gangster's Mercedes?

6. How did the Holy Spirit show up when Roma went to his mother's church?

7. Pastor Cymbala says the church is meant to be "a Holy Ghost hospital." What does this colorful image evoke in your mind? What would that look like?

Are there times in your life when you feel the need to be a "patient" in such a hospital? Explain.

After you've watched the video segment of the Brooklyn Tabernacle Choir singing "I Need You Once Again," pray in any of the following directions:

- Thank Jesus for sending his Spirit to live within us—we are not alone!

- Thank the Spirit for the things he has done for us in the past and is doing for us now. Be specific.

- Ask the Spirit to frequently remind us that he is at work in the world and ask him what we might do to be his agents of love, grace, and healing.

- Pray that every group member would yield themselves to the Holy Spirit's work inside them in the coming week.

"Whatever God is doing in our world today, he is doing through the Holy Spirit. He has no other agent on this planet."

Fresh Power, *p. 192*

Pastor Cymbala talked about the effect of the Holy Spirit on a fisherman named Peter. Over this coming week, read (or skim) the following eighteen episodes from Peter's life. Jot down a one-line description of what each is about (see first example), and then give Peter a numerical rating (0–10) on how he's doing spiritually. In other words, to what extent is he fulfilling what God has in mind for him?

	Scripture	What's Happening?	Rating (0 = pathetic, 10 = outstanding)
A	Matthew 14:22–33	*Walking on the lake*	
B	John 6:60–69		
C	Matthew 16:21–23		
D	Matthew 17:1–8		
E	Matthew 26:31–35		
F	Matthew 26:36–41		
G	John 18:2–11		
H	Matthew 26:69–75		

	Scripture	What's Happening?	Rating (0 = pathetic, 10 = outstanding)
I	Luke 24:9–12		
J	John 21:1–22		
JESUS LEAVES; THE HOLY SPIRIT COMES			
K	Acts 2:14–41		
L	Acts 3		
M	Acts 4:1–20		
N	Acts 8:14–25		
O	Acts 9:32–42		
P	Acts 10		
Q	Acts 15:6–11		
R	Letters of 1 Peter, 2 Peter		

Now transfer your ratings to the chart on the next page, in order to see the overall pattern. Put a dot on the grid to represent each rating for each episode in Peter's life. Connect the dots from left to right with a solid line.

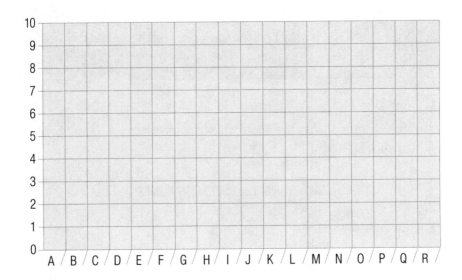

What does this tell you about the Holy Spirit's effect on one ordinary person?

Power Source

Paul: "I pray that out of [God's] glorious riches he may strengthen you with power through his Spirit in your inner being."

(Ephesians 3:16)

Have you ever experienced an electrical blackout? If so, how long did it last? What was it like for you?

Notes

As you watch the session two video, use the following outline to jot down any ideas that stand out to you.

Our job is not to "figure everything out."

The early Christians: great results in spite of weak credentials

Having the *right message* isn't enough.

Ebbs and flows throughout church history

1 Corinthians 12:7 — "To each one the manifestation of the Spirit is given for the common good."

The Terry Khem story

"New" is not always good.

"I believe, and am growing more into this belief, that divine, miraculous, creative power resides in the Holy Spirit.... Unless He attend the Word in power, vain will be the attempt in preaching it. Human eloquence or persuasiveness of speech are the mere trappings of the dead."

Evangelist Dwight L. Moody at a prayer convocation,
Northfield, Mass., 1880

1. Why do you think Jesus didn't let his trained disciples "get to work" immediately in sharing the good news around Jerusalem? Weren't they fully informed about the gospel? What was the significance of his telling them to *wait*?

2. The Holy Spirit is more than just a "nice guy," a friendly agent (as we discussed in session one). He is our only power source. Read the following New Testament verses and briefly note how the words "Spirit" (or "Holy Spirit") and "power" are tied together.

    a. Luke 1:35

    b. Luke 4:14

    c. Acts 1:8

    d. Acts 10:38

    e. Romans 1:4

cont.

f. Romans 15:13, 18 – 19

g. 1 Corinthians 2:4

h. 1 Corinthians 12:8 – 10

i. Galatians 4:29

j. Ephesians 3:16

k. 1 Thessalonians 1:5

l. 2 Timothy 1:7

"Do we need more translations of the Bible? Do we need
more praise-and-worship choruses? Do we need better
sound systems in our churches? Better choir risers? Better
lighting? Do we need to serve more coffee before the service?
What we *really* need is something from heaven."

From the video

3. Which one of the verses from question 2 stands out the most to you? Why?

> "We are in urgent need of some manifestation,
> some demonstration, of the power of the Holy Spirit."
>
> *British evangelical leader D. Martyn Lloyd-Jones,*
> *in a 1970s sermon at Westminster Chapel, London*

4. When Jim Cymbala talked about the importance of "something from heaven," what went through your mind?

5. Read 1 Corinthians 12:7 again. Pastor Cymbala applies this not just to the clergy but to each individual Christian. Can this be true? If so, what would it mean in today's context?

6. How did you see the manifestation of the Spirit's power in drawing a troubled woman such as Terry Khem?

After rewatching the final minute-and-a-half of the session two video, end your time together by praying in any of the following directions:

- Praise God that his power — the power of the Holy Spirit — is stronger than our weakness.
- Ask the Spirit to remind us regularly that apart from him we can do nothing.
- Pray that once again every group member would sense the Spirit's power and direction as they go about their lives the coming week, that they would act in that power for the "common good."

"And then it was, in the latter part of December [1734], that the Spirit of God began extraordinarily to set in, and wonderfully to work amongst us. There were, very suddenly, one after another, five or six persons who were to all appearance savingly converted, and some of them [were affected] in a very remarkable manner.... A great and earnest concern about the great things of religion and the eternal world became universal in all parts of the town, and among persons of all degrees and all ages. The noise amongst the dry bones waxed louder and louder.... More than three hundred souls were savingly brought home to Christ in this town, in the space of half a year.... The Spirit of God has so much extended not only His awakening, but regenerating influences."

Jonathan Edwards, pastor of the Congregational Church, Northampton, Mass., early hub of the First Great Awakening

Power for what? This week, give your attention to what the power of the Spirit accomplishes. Read the following Bible texts, taking notice of the various benefits that were realized:

Occurrence of the Spirit's power on display	What happened? How were people affected?
Peter's bold sermon: Acts 2, esp. vv. 32–41	
A prayer meeting: Acts 4:23–31	
The apostles' reply in court: Acts 5:27–42	
Stephen's public ministry: Acts 6:5–10; also 7:54–60	
Philip's side trip toward the desert: Acts 8:26–40	
Peter's introduction to Gentiles: Acts 10:9–23, 34–48	

Occurrence of the Spirit's power on display	What happened? How were people affected?
Agabus' prophecy: Acts 11:27–30	
Leadership meeting in Antioch: Acts 13:1–4	
Confrontation with an occultist: Acts 13:5–12	
Paul and Barnabas on the road: Acts 14:1–20	
Trip planning and adjustments: Acts 16:6–10	

The Best Bible Teacher

Jesus after the Last Supper: "I have much more to say to you, more than you can now bear. But when he, the Spirit of truth, comes, he will guide you into all the truth. He will not speak on his own; he will speak only what he hears, and he will tell you what is yet to come. He will glorify me because it is from me that he will receive what he will make known to you."

(John 16:12–14)

If you could send the Holy Spirit an email with just one question about the Book he inspired (the Bible), what would it be?

<u>Video Teaching Segment</u>

Notes

As you watch the session three video, use the following outline to jot down any ideas that stand out to you.

The difference a great teacher makes

A teacher (rabbi) better than Jesus?

More than "just reading"

1 John 2:26–27—"I am writing these things to you about those who are trying to lead you astray. As for you, the anointing you received from him remains in you, and you do not need anyone to teach you. But as his anointing teaches you about all things and as that anointing is real, not counterfeit—just as it has taught you, remain in him."

Read with open eyes; don't just reinforce prejudices.

We need Holy Spirit teaching, not our tradition—John 5:39–40.

Song: "Spirit of the living God, fall fresh on me ..."

The Brian Pettrey story

Group Discussion and Bible Study

1. Jim Cymbala talked early in the video about reading a familiar
   passage of Scripture for maybe the twentieth time — and then
   having a floodlight come on suddenly to show its true meaning.
   Has that ever happened to you? Tell the group about it.

2. What (or who) do you think turns the switch on this floodlight? What's really happening in such a circumstance? Why didn't we see the truth the first nineteen times?

3. Open your Bible to 1 Corinthians 2, the chapter that was mentioned at the end of the video. Read verses 1–5. Then discuss: What's going on here inside of Paul, who we know was an educated man with strong communication skills? What is he telling us? What might this signal to ordinary Christians such as you and me?

"The Spirit of God will never contradict himself. When we test everything by the Word of God, we are doing nothing more or less than honoring again the Holy Spirit who authored it."

Fresh Power, *p. 29*

4. Read verses 6 – 10a. What are the differences between "the wisdom of this age" (v. 6) and "God's wisdom" (v. 7)? Name several.

How do we tap into that divine wisdom?

5. Read verses 10b – 13. Rephrase verse 12 in your own words to make it more personal. What would be the result of truly believing what this verse affirms?

6. Read verses 14–16. Who is verse 14 talking about? Can you illustrate (without naming names)?

7. The quotation in verse 16 (from Isaiah 40:13) seems to say we can never hope to catch on to what God is thinking. But how does the last line ("We have the mind of Christ") modify that?

8. What role did the Scriptures play in turning eighteen-year-old Brian Pettrey in a new direction?

"If we don't get help from the Holy Spirit, we can fall into the terrible habit of reading Scripture only to find more ammunition for what we already believe. We need to come instead like children."

From the video

Closing Prayer and Meditation

To practice the message of this session, first pray as a group that the Holy Spirit, our Teacher, will illuminate the words of Scripture as only he can. Perhaps you might use phrases from Psalm 119, such as "Open my eyes that I may see wonderful things in your law" (v. 18) or "Direct me in the path of your commands, for there I find delight" (v. 35).

Then individually (and silently) read Psalm 23, as if for the very first time, and allow the Spirit to teach you from this timeless passage.

Finally, after a few minutes of meditation, share as a group what you heard from the psalm. What did you see? What did the Holy Spirit bring alive to you?

"Thousands stand ready to split doctrinal hairs and instruct others in the fine meaning of Scripture words — but there are so few through whom the Holy Spirit can work to bring [people] to new birth in the kingdom of God."

William Law, English devotional writer, 1761

Continue the "Spirit-tutored" approach to reading and receiving from Scripture that you practiced in the group. In fact, put it to use on some of the other ultra-familiar chapters of the Bible. Ask the Holy Spirit to shine his light on the page as you read and wait before him. Take notes on what he reveals to your mind and heart.

- Psalm 139

- Isaiah 40

- Matthew 5

- 1 Corinthians 13

- James 1

Water, Wind, and Fire

John answered them all, "I baptize you with water. But one who is more powerful than I will come, the straps of whose sandals I am not worthy to untie. He will baptize you with the Holy Spirit and fire."

(Luke 3:16)

On a scale of 1 to 10, from *gentle* to *boisterous*, where would you place the Holy Spirit, and why?

Video Teaching Segment

Notes

As you watch the session four video, use the following outline to jot down any ideas that stand out to you.

Various symbols of the Holy Spirit

No water = no life

More than a trickle

Hosea 14:5 — "I will be like the dew to Israel; he will blossom like a lily."

Acts 3:19 — "Turn to God, so that ... times of refreshing may come from the Lord."

Fire *penetrates.*

"Unless the water of the Holy Spirit comes, there's no life in us or in our churches. Without the Holy Spirit, you can have perfect ortho-doxy — your doctrine can be right — but there's still just death."

From the video

Fire *illuminates.*

Fire is *contagious.*

Angel Zapata's story

Let the divine fire burn up our unneeded confetti!

1. Read Jesus' bold proclamation at the temple in John 7:37–39. How is water an apt symbol or metaphor for what the Holy Spirit does?

2. Why do you think Jesus spoke about "streams/rivers" of the Spirit instead of, say, "reservoirs" or "pools"?

3. Did you understand Pastor Cymbala's treatment of the unusual symbol of dew? If so, what does it signify to you?

    If you can recall a similar experience to Cymbala's time in the attic, briefly describe it.

"The water of God's Spirit is absolutely free, but we must wait by faith continually to receive fresh infillings of this promise from the Father."

Fresh Power, p. 200

4. Which of the three properties of fire (it penetrates, it illuminates, it's contagious) especially spoke to you? In what way?

5. In 1 Thessalonians 5:19 the apostle Paul writes, "Do not quench the Spirit." How might we Christians do that unintentionally today?

"Fire burns up anything that's superfluous. And that's what the Holy Spirit does in our lives.... His fire illuminates our choices so we know what to avoid. The Holy Spirit was sent to guide us in the path we need to take."

From the video

6. Angel Zapata told about a dramatic encounter in the classroom with the Holy Spirit's fire. What did this fire burn out of him as a result? How is he different today?

After you listen to the audio clip, "God Is Moving by His Spirit," by the Brooklyn Tabernacle Choir (sing along if you'd like), take turns praying, using the symbols of the Spirit—breath, oil, water, dew, and fire—as your theme.

"The power of Christ's dispensation is a fiery pulpit — not a learned pulpit, not a popular pulpit, not an eloquent pulpit, but a pulpit on fire with the Holy Ghost.... This power is not the mere iteration or reiteration of truth well learned or well told, but it is the enabling force to declare revealed truth with superhuman authority.... This power is from the Holy Ghost singular and alone."

E. M. Bounds (1835–1913),
Civil War veteran and Methodist pastor

Spend time this week probing the two other symbols of the Holy Spirit that Pastor Cymbala mentioned briefly at the start.

Holy Spirit as Wind/Breath

All three English words *breath, wind,* and *spirit* (or *Spirit)* relate to the Greek word *pneuma,* from which we get our word *pneumatic;* all sorts of pneumatic tools, from dentists' drills to jackhammers, run on air pressure. We also know about *pneumonia,* i.e., when your "wind" isn't moving very well.

Here are some biblical sections about the Holy Spirit that use some form of *pneuma* (or the Hebrew equivalent, *ruach).* Write your own observations about the connection.

- Creation: Genesis 1:1 – 2

- The valley of dry bones: Ezekiel 37:1 – 14

- Jesus' explanation to Nicodemus: John 3:5 – 8

- Easter night: John 20:19 – 22

- The upper room: Acts 2:1 – 2 and following

Holy Spirit as Oil

Olive oil for anointing purposes was a very big thing in the Old Testament (see Exodus 30:22–33 for the elaborate formula). It was used, among other things, to formally designate both priests and kings for future service. New Testament usage of oil continued to show the Spirit's anointing.

Look for the linkage to the Holy Spirit in these Scriptures:

- The prophet Samuel comes to Jesse's house: 1 Samuel 16:1–13

- The prophet Isaiah foretells about the coming Messiah: Isaiah 61:1–3

- Jesus cites the Isaiah prophecy in his inaugural message at the Nazareth synagogue: Luke 4:14–21

- Peter explains to a Gentile audience what made Jesus so special: Acts 10:36–38

- Paul explains how believers stand firm in Christ: 2 Corinthians 1:21–22

- James explains one way the Spirit's power to heal is released: James 5:13–16

Who's in Control?

Then [Jesus] opened their minds so they could understand the Scriptures. He told them, "This is what is written: The Messiah will suffer and rise from the dead on the third day, and repentance for the forgiveness of sins will be preached in his name to all nations, beginning at Jerusalem. You are witnesses of these things. I am going to send you what my Father has promised; but stay in the city until you have been clothed with power from on high."

(Luke 24:45–49)

Most of us resent the idea of being controlled by another person. But can you think of cases where that's a *good* thing?

Video Teaching Segment

Notes

As you watch the session five video, use the following outline to jot down any ideas that stand out to you.

"Son of Sam"

What does it mean to be "filled with the Spirit"?

Are *all* Christians *always* filled?

The main point of Ephesians 5:17 – 18

An example: Stephen

"A failure to realize that our salvation can only be worked out by the power of the indwelling Holy Spirit ... has placed the Christian church today in the same apostasy that characterized the Jewish nation. And it has occurred for one and the same reason. The Jews refused Him who was the substance and fulfilling of all that was taught in their Law and Prophets. The Christian church is in a fallen state for the same rejection of the Holy Spirit, who was given to be the power and fulfilling of all that was promised by the gospel. And just as the Pharisees' rejection of Christ was [based on] a profession of faith in the Messianic Scriptures, so church leaders today reject the demonstration and power of the Holy Spirit in the name of sound doctrine."

William Law, English devotional writer, 1761

Our current need

Todd Crews

Infilling can't be *taught*.

1. Read the following New Testament examples of being filled with the Spirit, completing the chart as you proceed.

Reference	Who was filled?	Already believers in Christ, or not?
Acts 2:1–4		
Acts 4:31		
Acts 8:14–17		
Acts 10:44–48		
Acts 13:49–52		
Acts 19:1–7		

2. Why do you think the first deacons needed to be "full of the Spirit and wisdom" (Acts 6:3)? Weren't they mainly selected just to organize meals for the church widows?

3. But then Stephen, one of the deacons, expanded his work far beyond "kitchen duty." Quickly scan from Acts 6:8 through 7:60, and point out what you see him doing in the Spirit's power.

4. Look carefully at Ephesians 5:17 – 18. How is being Spirit-filled the opposite of being intoxicated?

"The Ephesians 5:18 sentence 'Be filled with the Spirit' is more than a command; it is phrased in the continuous present tense, so that some translations render it literally, 'Be being filled with the Spirit' or 'Keep on being filled with the Holy Spirit.'"

From the video

5. Pastor Cymbala says that to be Spirit-filled is to be *Spirit-controlled*. Does that shed new light for you on this dimension? If so, how?

6. In what ways did you notice the Holy Spirit controlling the life and actions of Todd Crews?

7. When Todd became frustrated with menial library work, the Holy Spirit seemed to say to him, "It's not about what you're doing; it's about what you're becoming." What do you sense the Holy Spirit wants *you* to become?

"David Berkowitz has become a dear friend to Carol and me. Not only that, but he is my brother in Christ, for God has changed the very 'chief of sinners' — a demon-controlled serial killer — into a precious child of God."

From the book Fresh Power, *which tells the full* "Son of Sam" *testimony on pp. 130–136*

Instead of praying as a group, spend some time alone waiting on the Lord. If possible, do so in a different part of the house, building, or even outdoors, and in a posture (sitting, kneeling, standing, walking) that is most comfortable for you. Ask the Holy Spirit to come in his fullness and control you; open your heart and soul to his coming.

"In our times, don't you think we need a revival of people being filled with the Holy Spirit? Don't we need something to offset the powers of the world that are encroaching upon us and into our children's lives? Do we have to just roll along and feel defeated as we see our families broken apart? Doesn't God have any kind of antidote?"

From the video

The 120 believers in the upper room waited a total of ten days for the Holy Spirit's coming (Acts 1:12–2:1). What did they do all that time?

A brief period was spent in choosing a new apostle, Matthias, to replace Judas. But most of the time, they simply "all joined together constantly in prayer" (Acts 1:14). Hour after hour, day after day, they waited before the Lord, anticipating the promise Jesus had made to them. They eagerly wanted the Holy Spirit to come and fill them with his power and presence. They could think of nothing more important to capture their attention.

Over the next seven days of *your* life, before the next group meeting, find a quiet place and give yourself repeatedly to prayer for the fullness of the Holy Spirit. Ask him to come and control you—your mind, your thoughts, your motives, your various forms of service to God's kingdom. Be open to whatever he wants to do in your life. The original disciples didn't know what to expect, but they were open.

You don't need to feel pressured to constantly verbalize sentences and paragraphs to God. You can simply wait in passive mode, listening for his voice. Some of the deepest spiritual experiences happen without planning or programming.

While no doubt you have daily responsibilities that will pull you away during this week, keep coming back to this place of prayer. Let your attitude and even your posture convey the desire of "Come, Holy Spirit—I need you. Do everything in me that you know would be best."

Feel free to record any insights from these experiences on the next two pages.

Help When We Need It Most

In the same way, the Spirit helps us in our weakness. We do not know what we ought to pray for, but the Spirit himself intercedes for us through wordless groans. And he who searches our hearts knows the mind of the Spirit, because the Spirit intercedes for God's people in accordance with the will of God.

(Romans 8:26–27)

All of us like to feel "on top of things" in life, spiritually and in every other way. But when have you felt *most inadequate* as a Christian? (It's okay—you can be honest!)

Notes

As you watch the session six video, use the following outline to jot down any ideas that stand out to you.

The Brooklyn Tabernacle's "engine"

"Saying prayers" vs. praying from your heart in faith

What does "Spirit-filled" look like?

Vital signs from Acts 2:42 – 47

A Spirit-filled church (or person) is . . .

When you *don't* feel like praying

Two ways the Spirit helps us pray:

_____

_____

Diana Barrios set free

"When the Spirit of God is working, he always guides us to the throne of grace. How? By constantly revealing to us our weakness and failure — where we're not acting like Christ. Others might be patting us on the back; the Holy Spirit instead shows us our need of Christ and leads us in that direction."

From the video

1. When in your own experience have life's pressures grown so strong that you felt *driven* to prayer?

2. Turn back to the start of this session (page 63) and read the Scripture (Romans 8:26–27). Like Paul, have you ever felt at a loss for words while praying? What happened then? Tell the story.

3. Pastor Cymbala draws a strong link between a church's prayer life and its awareness of the Holy Spirit. How so? What's the connection there?

"God's first people were not called 'Jews' or 'the children of Israel' or 'Hebrews.' In the *very* beginning their original name was 'those who call on the name of the LORD' (see Genesis 4:26). On some unmarked day ... at some unnoted hour ... a God-placed instinct in human hearts came alive. People sensed that if you are in trouble and you call out to God, he will answer you! He will intervene in your situation."

Fresh Wind, Fresh Fire, *p. 54*

4. In two different epistles, the Bible urges us to *pray in the Spirit* (Ephesians 6:18; Jude 20). What do you think this means?

5. How would *you* have reacted the night Diana Barrios showed up in church? Was this scene any different from what happened to Jesus or the apostles? (See, for example, Mark 1:21–28; Luke 9:37–43; Acts 8:4–8; Acts 13:4–12.)

6. As this study comes to an end, what is your greatest desire regarding the Holy Spirit? In what way do you most want to see him move in your life and situation?

"Since you were here I have been thinking of prayer — particularly of praying for the Holy Ghost and its descent. It seems to me that I have always limited God in this request.... I am now convinced, it is my duty and privilege, and the duty of every other Christian, to pray for as much of the Holy Spirit as came down on the day of Pentecost, and a great deal more. I know not why we may not ask for the entire and utmost influence of the Spirit to come down, and, asking in faith, see the full answer."

Last letter written by Daniel Nash, little-known prayer partner of Presbyterian evangelist Charles G. Finney, before Nash's death in 1831

After listening to the audio clip of the Brooklyn Tabernacle congregation singing the chorus, "Come, Holy Spirit, O How I Need You," sing it in your group as well. Then end the session by lifting this same prayer to God in your own words. Ask for the Spirit's outpouring on you, your group, your church, your city. Ask him for the strength to be "doers of the Word," not just hearers.

"God is not dead; he's still alive. And what he's done through the centuries when people have prayed, he can still do today. Let's ask the Holy Spirit to come and grant us a new spirit of prayer in our churches, in our small groups, and in our individual lives."

From the video

The Bible gives us several examples of desperate people pouring out their hearts to the Lord, as the Holy Spirit enabled both fervency and faith. Take these one at a time; read the account, noticing the passion engendered by the Spirit.

Then adapt each prayer to your own voice. Call on the name of the Lord for yourself. Implore him to meet your needs, and praise him for his answers to come.

The Bible Passage(s)	The Bible Prayer
1 Sam. 1:9 – 20; 2:1 – 10	Hannah's prayer for a child — and subsequent response
Ps. 51, esp. v. 11	David's prayer after making a stupid mistake
2 Kings 19:14 – 19	Hezekiah's prayer when under attack
Dan. 9:1 – 19	Daniel's prayer for those in tough times
Acts 4:23 – 31	The Jerusalem church after being seriously harassed
Eph. 1:15 – 23; Phil. 1:3 – 11; Col. 1:9 – 12	Paul's prayers from prison

Appendix

NOTE: The following chapter is reprinted with permission from Jim Cymbala's bestselling book on the Holy Spirit, *Fresh Power* (Zondervan, 2001).

A Long Night in Indianapolis

In the fall of 1994 I was invited to speak at a Christian music gathering in Indianapolis. I had visited once before, so I knew that some 10,000 people came mainly to hear great gospel singing. Yes, there was a speaker each morning and also a number of workshops throughout the day, but the drawing card of the event was the musical praise and worship.

I arrived on a Thursday, and that evening I still wasn't sure what I should speak about the next morning. I was leaning toward a simple message of encouragement—one I had preached before. I thought it would go well in this festive setting. I certainly didn't want to do anything controversial or get in anybody's face about anything. On this, my first chance to speak to this large gathering, my human nature wanted to be liked and accepted.

I went to part of the evening concert with my daughter and son-in-law, Chrissy and Al Toledo, but left around eight o'clock to return to my hotel room. There I began to seek the Lord about my message for the next morning. I knew that out of the thousands of good Bible verses a preacher could profitably use, there must be one passage that the Lord specifically had in mind for that occasion and that audience. Over the years I've tried to pray along these lines before speaking, asking God not only for his anointing but also for a confirmation of the subject for each occasion.

I reviewed my sermon outline and then went to prayer. After all, I knew I needed his help for this message to prove a blessing to the people.

Off Track

The longer I prayed, the more this nice, familiar sermon idea went dead inside of me. There was no stirring in my heart. The outline was biblical enough, to be sure, and no doubt the people would be helped by it. But I knew it wasn't the right fit. Something else was waiting in the wings for me. And to be honest, I didn't really want to find out what it was.

I kept praying. In time I felt drawn toward the text "My house will be called a house of prayer" (Mark 11:17), a message I had preached not long before at the Brooklyn Tabernacle. It's a very direct message. It deals with Jesus' cleaning the merchants out of the temple and pointedly calls the audience to what the church is really for, as opposed to all the misuses we make of it. (This message later became part of my first book as a chapter entitled "The Day Jesus Got Mad.")

"God, I'm not a regular speaker at this gathering. I have no right to stand up and confront these people. They'll be sitting there thinking, *Who does he think he is—some New York City wise guy? This is starting to sound like a revival service.* They didn't invite me here to stir up controversy. If I tell them that today's church has become prayerless and is in danger of Jesus coming in judgment . . . well, this is hardly the way to win friends and influence people."

It was getting late. I had no notes for that message anyway. I could remember only parts and pieces of what I had preached at home. Surely I wasn't going to get up in front of 10,000 people and just "wing it."

Yet the Holy Spirit seemed to persistently whisper to my heart, *This is why I brought you here. This is what I want you to preach. Are you going to do my will, or are you just going to go out there tomorrow morning and "perform"?*

I kept struggling in prayer. This whole situation was getting messy. If I didn't get my act together soon and get some sleep, I was headed for a big embarrassment. Why couldn't I just follow through on what I had planned?

On the other hand, if I went against what God wanted me to do, I would fail the Lord who called me into the ministry.

Finally, after an hour or two, I relented. I opened my Bible to the passage in Mark as I said, "God, help me. If you want to use this to speak to the people tomorrow morning, all right. Show me how to reconstruct this sermon."

Around midnight something very unusual happened. I'm normally not a timid person, but on this night I was attacked by a tremendous feeling of fear and insecurity. I began to imagine the audience turning against me. Something or someone kept whispering to me that this "prophetic" message wasn't going to fit the setting at all. It seemed as if I was battling against forces intent on disrupting this message I now felt so strongly.

My heart began to pound. I started pacing around the room. Before long, I was crying. "O God, now that you've shown me your will, and I'm willing to do it — give me the courage, the power, the wisdom to preach this message for your glory."

I turned out the light and tried to get some sleep, but couldn't. Soon I was back up again, pacing and praying. I kept battling an ominous sense that this whole thing was going to be a disaster. Finally, around three-thirty I fell asleep out of sheer exhaustion.

The sun had just come up that Friday morning when the telephone rang. It wasn't my wake-up call from the hotel desk; it was my wife, Carol, back in New York. "Jim, are you okay?" she asked with a worried tone.

"Yes, I think so," I answered groggily.

"What's going on there with you?" she persisted.

"Well, the truth is, I'm in a battle," I admitted. "I have to speak in a couple of hours, and the Lord's been dealing with me about a message that's not easy to preach. I'm really struggling."

"I knew something was wrong," she replied. "I couldn't sleep last night. I woke up and had to intercede for you. I didn't know what was going on, but somehow I was really burdened for you." She then began praying for me right there on the phone.

When she finished, she added, "God's going to help you, Jim. Just depend on the Holy Spirit to help you, and let it go."

Into the Arena

I hung up the phone and, on less than four hours' sleep, began getting ready for the day ahead. All too soon I was across the street at the arena. The sound of all the people singing at the start of the morning session echoed through the corridors.

Someone came to put the clip-on microphone on my tie. That was my first signal that I wouldn't have the usual hand-held mike, which is what I'm most comfortable with when I speak because it gives me something to do with one hand. Worse than that — the audiovisual technician reminded me that I would be on a center stage in the round, with people on all sides, which meant I would have to remember to keep turning continually to face new sections, one after another. And a set of video cameras would be following me!

From my point of view, the circumstances could not have been more awkward.

As the host began to introduce me, I walked out onto the circle stage and nervously took stock of what I was up against. *O God, help me now!* I prayed silently.

I began speaking in a soft voice. "I want to talk for a few moments about something so vital, and yet it's so simple. It's so familiar to us—and that's the danger. I want our session this morning to be something that will make a difference in our lives....

"To approach this subject, I want to give you one of the most strange and stunning pictures of Jesus found anywhere in the Bible." I then began to describe Jesus' cleansing of the temple.

It seemed that the longer I spoke, the more clarity came into my heart. I felt calm inside. I could sense the Holy Spirit helping me. I kept walking and turning as I spoke, looking out into the sea of faces that stretched upward into shadows on all sides. Without notes, the logic and sequence of my remarks seemed to fall together. Even though I was saying some difficult things for people to hear—that gospel music had the potential to be mere entertainment rather than genuine ministry, for example—they seemed to respond. Their hearts were engaged.

My tone was not harsh or condescending. Instead, I expressed the cry of my own heart for more of God. The burden within me was transferred to those who listened. In time I came to feel almost removed from what was taking place. It was as if I was lifted up and watching the stage from one of the upper seats. All nervousness and self-consciousness were gone now. I was just pouring out what I felt God wanted me to say.

As I came to the end, I told the story of how desperate prayer had pulled our teenage daughter Chrissy back from rebellion and self-destruction to serve the Lord again. (In fact, Chrissy and her husband were now sitting there in the audience listening to me.) Some of the last sentences I uttered were, "God says that when you call, he will answer. The hard cases some of you are facing today—the answer won't come from another seminar.... We have too many mere technicians who are only stressing methodology, and they are increasingly invading the church. The answer is not in any human methodology. The answer is in the power of the Holy Spirit. The answer is in the grace of God." I then did something unusual for that type of gathering: I made a direct call for response.

There was very little area to use around the stage, so I simply had people stand who wanted to call upon God in prayer for situations that only God could help. Possibly they had given up because it seemed so hopeless: wayward children, spiritual weakness, marriages under siege. A number of them edged toward the center anyway and began to call upon the Lord, many with tears. "O God, intervene in my life and the crisis I'm facing," they prayed. "Have mercy upon us and stretch out your hand of power as you promised to do."

I walked off the stage, removed my tie-clip microphone, and was soon ushered to a car to return to the Indianapolis airport. Some of the folks shook my hand and thanked me. Inside, I felt peace: God had indeed helped me do what he wanted in that place.

Ripples in the Water

During the next few months I chatted occasionally with my friend who had invited me, and he mentioned that sales of that morning's video were beyond any in their previous experience. A year later, even after two or three years, the video continued to sell and to spread all across the country by word of mouth.

Reports came of ministerial groups watching it in faraway places. Faxes and e-mails continually arrived. A conference of more than 2,000 people in New England watched it during a main session, and when the tape ended, a prayer meeting broke out as people spontaneously went to the throne of grace.

More than one pastor called to say, "I don't know you personally, but I just wanted you to know that I showed your video in my first morning service—and the people got up en masse to come pray at the altar, which is not the custom in our church. When it was time for them to clear out so the next crowd could come in for the next service, I didn't know what to do.... The new people just came in and joined the first group in calling upon God and waiting in his presence."

A godly revival ministry in Michigan was blessed by a donor who paid for thousands of copies to go to spiritually hungry pastors. Great reports kept coming back of what transpired—*all because the Lord took over my plans in a hotel room and showed me his will*. I hadn't wanted to preach that message at all. But God knew exactly why he had me there.

When I think back to that long night in Indianapolis, I think about Jesus' words in John 16:7: "I tell you the truth: It is for your good that I am going away. Unless I go away, the Counselor will not come to you; but if I go, I will send him to you."

This must have sounded very strange to the disciples. They had been at Jesus' side for more than three years; he was everything to them. They moved when he moved. He answered all their questions. When they were sad or apprehensive, he assured them. It was unthinkable that Jesus should ever leave them, or that this would be a *good* or even *better* thing.

But our Lord knew what was best. His statement highlighted the greatness of the Holy Spirit's coming ministry in their lives and the life of the Christian church. The Holy Spirit would be everything to them, even more than the physical Jesus had been. They would accomplish more under his direction and power than they had ever done in the time of Jesus. That is not blasphemous or degrading to Christ, because he said it himself.

Jesus had been with them, but he was *outside of them*. And the great work that needed to be done in the disciples was internal. This was at the very heart of the New Covenant that God was making with his people: "I will give you a new heart and put a new spirit in you; I will remove from you your heart of stone and give you a heart of flesh. And I will put my Spirit in you" (Ezekiel 36:26–27).

While Christ's work on the cross, the shedding of his blood, was the only way to settle the problem of guilt, sin, and condemnation, the coming of the promised Holy Spirit was God's way of changing human beings from the inside out. The law given to Moses had failed on this very point. It was in itself holy and just, but the problem was the sinful nature within people. Now the Holy Spirit dwelling in the hearts of believers would conquer the age-old dilemma of "I want to be different but can't. I know what's wrong—but I keep doing it anyway." This empowerment by the Spirit would be the dynamic source throughout time for all who live and labor for Jesus Christ.

Our Earnest Need

What happened to me in Indianapolis was not unusual. It was merely the Holy Spirit coming to the aid of a human vessel who didn't really know what he was supposed to be doing. The Spirit is the one who leads us into God's will. As Jesus had led and inspired his disciples while on earth, the Holy Spirit came to do the same in a more powerful, intimate way.

That night in the hotel room was a case of Romans 8:26, which boldly declares, "The Spirit helps us in our weakness. We do not know what we ought to pray for, but the Spirit himself intercedes for us with groans that words cannot express."

Today this is one of the most neglected truths in the whole New Testament. We Christians seldom admit that we don't know how to pray. Many of us have been taught since childhood how to put sentences together that sound like a prayer, to the point that we are professionals at it. Some can turn out an eloquent presentation to God at a moment's notice.

Prayer born of the Spirit, however, is another dimension of calling on God to the point of having the Holy Spirit supernaturally assist us. This is not a worked-up emotionalism but a powerful promise of help from God himself! The Holy Spirit helped me to pray as I struggled in weakness that night.

The alarm that went off in Carol's heart to pray for me was also a supernatural assistance from the Holy Spirit. He is able to communicate knowledge through other than the natural senses. Carol knew I needed prayer and intercession even though no one had told her of my dilemma—no one, that is, but the omniscient Spirit of God. So she lifted up fervent petitions, going far beyond any mechanical, routine prayer.

The boldness that I needed to go beyond myself in a very intimidating situation came only through the Holy Spirit. He lifted me above my natural fears and verbal limitations. I'm no natural orator, let me assure you. Only the enablement of the Spirit made those words come across with clarity and impact. But this is the very reason that the Spirit has come: to inspire and equip ordinary people to work for Jesus Christ.

Almost a hundred years ago in England, a Methodist leader and college president named Samuel Chadwick wrote:

> The work of God is not by might of men or by the power of men but by his Spirit. It is by him the truth convicts and converts, sanctifies and saves. The philosophies of men fail, but the Word of God in the demonstration of the Spirit prevails. Our wants are many, and our faults innumerable, but they are all comprehended in our lack of the Holy Ghost. We want nothing but the fire.
>
> The resources of the church are in "the supply of the Spirit." The Spirit is more than the minister of consolation. He is Christ without the limitations of the flesh and the material world. He can reveal what Christ could not speak. He has resources of power greater than those Christ could use, and he makes possible greater works than his. He is the Spirit of God, the Spirit of truth, the Spirit of witness, the Spirit of conviction, the Spirit of power, the Spirit of holiness, the Spirit of light, the Spirit of adoption, the Spirit of help, the Spirit of liberty, the Spirit of wisdom, the Spirit of revelation, the Spirit of promise, the Spirit of love, the Spirit of meekness, the Spirit of sound mind, the Spirit of grace, the Spirit of glory, and the Spirit of prophecy. It is for the church to explore the resources of the Spirit; the resources of the world are futile.*

This "supply of the Spirit" (Philippians 1:19 KJV) is the great need of our hour. We are currently living in the era of the Holy Spirit as we await the return of our Savior Jesus Christ. Our Lord

---

*Samuel Chadwick, *The Way to Pentecost* (reprint, Dixon, Mo.: Rare Christian Books, n.d.), 19.

is seated at the Father's right hand in heaven, but he has sent the promised Spirit so that, through his power, we can fulfill all of God's will, defeat every device of Satan, and extend the kingdom of Christ here on earth.

No matter what difficulties confront us as believers or as local congregations, God is calling us to receive today this great promise of power as a living reality. Then in victory we will praise God alongside those believers down through the ages who have experienced for themselves the truth that "greater is he that is in you, than he that is in the world" (1 John 4:4 KJV).

When God's People Pray DVD Curriculum

Six Sessions on the Transforming Power of Prayer

Jim Cymbala, Bestselling Author
of Fresh Wind, Fresh Fire

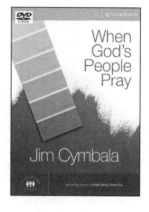

Prayer can change lives and circumstances like nothing else can. What are the keys that unlock its power, that turn prayer from a mere activity into a vital link with God and all his resources? In this DVD with separate participant's guide, Jim Cymbala, pastor of Brooklyn Tabernacle, shows you and your small group truths about prayer that God has used to turn his own church from a tiny, struggling inner-city congregation into a vital, thriving community of believers who pray with passion, focus, and faith.

Featuring teachings by Jim Cymbala and video interviews of ordinary people who have received extraordinary answers to their prayers, these six sessions will help you pray with new confidence.

Six sessions include:

1. God's Heart for Us
2. The Amazing Power of Prayer
3. Obedience in Prayer
4. The Word of God and Prayer
5. Why Prayer Matters
6. Creating a Prayer Ministry in Your Church

Available in stores and online!

ZONDERVAN®
.com

Fresh Wind, Fresh Fire

What Happens When God's Spirit Invades the Hearts of His People

Jim Cymbala with Dean Merrill

In 1972 the Brooklyn Tabernacle's spark was almost out. Then the Holy Spirit lit a fire that couldn't be quenched.

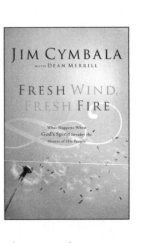

Pastor Jim Cymbala shares the lessons he learned when the Spirit ignited his heart and began to move through his people. This unforgettable story will set a fire burning in your own heart to experience God's mercy, power, and love as though for the first time.

> "This is an important book for all those whose Christianity has become still and sterile. *Fresh Wind, Fresh Fire* signals that God is at work in our day and that he wishes to be at work in our lives."
>
> —DR. JOSEPH M. STOWELL

> "This book will drive you to your knees. Be prepared to be provoked but also greatly challenged. You can be sure that reading this book will change you forever."
>
> —DAVID WILKERSON

Pick up a copy today at your favorite bookstore!

ZONDERVAN®
.com

Fresh Faith

What Happens When Real Faith Ignites God's People

Jim Cymbala with Dean Merrill

Like a Fountain of Clear Water Cleansing a Stagnant, Cynical Culture . . .

FRESH FAITH

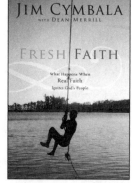

Pastor Jim Cymbala calls us back to a fiery, passionate preoccupation with God that will restore what the enemy has stolen from us: our first love for Jesus, our zeal, our troubled children, our wounded marriages, our broken and divided churches.

Born out of the heart and soul of the Brooklyn Tabernacle, the message of *Fresh Faith* is illustrated by true stories of men and women whose lives have been changed through the power of faith.

The same faith that can transform your life—starting today, if you choose.

Pick up a copy today at your favorite bookstore!

Fresh Power

Experiencing the Vast Resources of the Spirit of God

Jim Cymbala with Dean Merrill

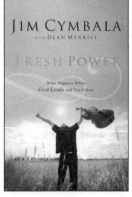

Pastor Jim Cymbala of the Brooklyn Taber-nacle has taught his congregation how God's mighty power can infuse their present-day lives and the mission of their church. He con-tinued that teaching nationally in his bestsell-ing books *Fresh Wind, Fresh Fire* and *Fresh Faith,* which tell about the transforming power of God's love to convert prostitutes, addicts, the homeless, and people of all races and sta-tions in life.

Now in *Fresh Power* Cymbala continues to spread the word about the power of God's Holy Spirit in the lives of those who seek him. Fresh power, Cymbala says, is available to us as we desire the Holy Spirit's constant infilling and learn what it means to be Spirit filled, both as individuals and as the church. With the book of Acts as the basis for his study, Cymbala shows how the daily lives of first-century Christians were defined by their belief in God's Word, in the constant infilling of his Spirit, and in the clear and direct responses of obedience to Scripture. He shows that that same life in Christ through the power of the Holy Spirit is available today for pas-tors, leaders, and laypeople who are longing for revival.

Pick up a copy today at your favorite bookstore!

ZONDERVAN®
.com

Breakthrough Prayer

The Secret of Receiving
What You Need from God

Jim Cymbala

**A practical and visionary approach to the
principles of prayer that will revolutionize
our lives — and enable us to receive all God has
for us.**

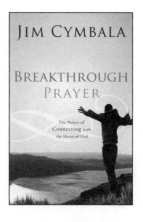

Many people are missing the great things
God wants to do in their lives because they
don't know how to receive answers to their
prayers. This revolutionary book is not a step-
by-step guide on how to pray but an inspiring
vision that moves people to greater hope as
they see the tremendous potential of prayer.

Breakthrough Prayer is peppered with amazing stories of answered
prayer from the Brooklyn Tabernacle, including the story of the final
survivor of the World Trade Center collapse and the prayers she
prayed before becoming the last person pulled from the wreckage
alive.

Unique features include:

- *Breakthrough to Holiness:* What is the connection between how
  we live and how we pray?
- *Breakthrough to Power:* What are the prayers that really have
  power with God?
- *Breakthrough to Listening:* How can we learn to recognize God's
  answers to our prayers?

Jesus said and did only the things he received from the Father.
When we do the same, the real potential of our lives will unfold, and
prayer will enable us to become people with instructed tongues who
are able to sustain others in fearful times — times much like those we
face today.

Share Your Thoughts

With the Author: Your comments will be forwarded to the author when you send them to *zauthor@zondervan.com*.

With Zondervan: Submit your review of this book by writing to *zreview@zondervan.com*.

Free Online Resources at
www.zondervan.com

Zondervan AuthorTracker: Be notified whenever your favorite authors publish new books, go on tour, or post an update about what's happening in their lives at www.zondervan.com/ authortracker.

Daily Bible Verses and Devotions: Enrich your life with daily Bible verses or devotions that help you start every morning focused on God. Visit www.zondervan.com/newsletters.

Free Email Publications: Sign up for newsletters on Christian living, academic resources, church ministry, fiction, children's resources, and more. Visit www.zondervan.com/newsletters.

Zondervan Bible Search: Find and compare Bible passages in a variety of translations at www.zondervanbiblesearch.com.

Other Benefits: Register yourself to receive online benefits like coupons and special offers, or to participate in research.

ZONDERVAN.com/
AUTHORTRACKER
follow your favorite authors